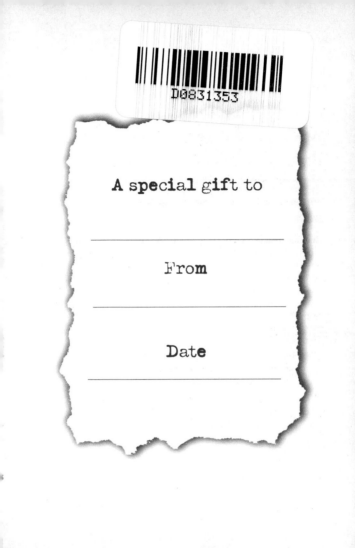

A special gift to

_____

From

_____

Date

_____

A Pocket Book of Prayers for Women

© 2004 Christian Art Gifts, RSA
        Christian Art Gifts Inc., IL, USA

Compiled by Lynette Douglas
Designed by Christian Art Gifts

Printed in Hong Kong

ISBN 1-86920-144-2

05   06   07   08   09   10   11   12   13   14   –   11   10   9   8   7   6   5   4

A Pocket Book of Prayers

for Women

christian
art gifts

Contents

The Lord's Prayer

Our Father in heaven,
hallowed be your name,
your kingdom come,
your will be done on earth
as it is in heaven.
Give us today our daily bread.
Forgive us our debts,
as we also have
forgiven our debtors.
And lead us not
into temptation,
but deliver us
from the evil one.

Matthew 6:9-13

Confession
and
Repentance

Cleansing and Purity

O Christ the Light,
illuminate and cleanse
the dark corners of the world
where hang the cobwebs of apathy
and the dust of neglect;
shine on faces made grim
by poverty and war;
melt the icicles of despair
and the hard frozen wastes
of selfishness;
and let Your searching rays
enclose the whole
in one great radiance.

Betty Hares

Dependence on God

Thank You, Lord,
for being the good
Father who gives
His children the joy of discovering
by themselves the treasures
of His intelligence and love,
but keep us from believing
that – by ourselves – we have
invented anything at all.
∽ Michel Quoist ∽

The Lord Knows

O LORD, you have searched me and you know me. You know when I sit and when I rise; you perceive my thoughts from afar. You discern my going out and my lying down; you are familiar with all my ways. Before a word is on my tongue you know it completely, O LORD. You hem me in – behind and before; you have laid your hand upon me. Such knowledge is too wonderful for me, too lofty for me to attain. How precious to me are your thoughts, O God! How vast is the sum of them! Were I to count them, they would outnumber the grains of sand. When I awake, I am still with you.

Psalm 139:1-6, 17-18

A Clean Heart

Father,
    Listen to my prayer.
    Turn my ways to Your ways;
    Make me holy,
    Set my thinking right;
    Straighten out my desires;
    Create a pure heart within me;
    Give me a new and steadfast spirit.
                Launcelot Andrewes

A Cheerful Spirit

Deliver me, O God,
from a slothful mind,
from all lukewarmness
and all dejection of spirit.
I know these cannot
but deaden my life to Thee;
mercifully free my heart from them,
and give me a lively,
zealous, active and cheerful spirit
that I may vigorously perform
whatever Thou commandest
and be ever ardent to obey
in all things Thy holy love.

∾ *John Wesley* ∾

The Way to Goodness

Lord, on the way to goodness,
when we stumble, hold us;
when we fall, lift us up;
when we are hard-pressed by evil,
deliver us;
when we turn from what is good,
turn us back;
and bring us at last to Thy glory.

Unknown

A Confession

In my attempts to promote the
comfort of my family, the quiet of my
spirit has been disturbed. Some of this is
doubtless owing to physical weakness;
but, with every temptation, there is a
way of escape; there is never any need
to sin. Another thing I have suffered
loss from – entering into the business
of the day without seeking to have
my spirit quieted and directed.
So many things press upon me, this is
sometimes neglected;
shame to me that this should be so.

This is of great importance, to watch carefully – now I am so weak – not over-fatigue myself, because then I cannot contribute to the pleasure of others. And a placid face and a gentle tone will make my family more happy than anything else I can do for them. Our own will gets sadly into the performance of our duties sometimes. Dear Lord, forgive me, and give me Your strength to perform Your will.
Amen

Elizabeth King

Spiritual
Growth

Strength of Love

I pray that out of his glorious riches
he may strengthen you
with power through his Spirit
in your inner being,
so that Christ may dwell
in your hearts through faith.
And I pray that you,
being rooted and established in love,
may have power,
together with all the saints,
to grasp how wide and long
and high and deep is the love of Christ,
and to know this love
that surpasses knowledge –
that you may be filled to the measure
of all the fullness of God.

Ephesians 3:16-19

Serving God

Teach us, Lord,
to serve You as You deserve,
to give and not to count the cost,
to fight and not to heed the wounds,
to toil and not to seek for rest,
to labor and not to ask for any reward
save that of knowing
that we do Your will.

⟡ Ignatius of Loyola ⟡

The Way of the Lord

Teach me your way, O LORD,
and I will walk in your truth;
give me an undivided heart,
that I may fear your name.
I will praise you, O LORD my God,
with all my heart;
I will glorify your name forever.
For great is your love toward me;
you have delivered me
from the depths of the grave.

Psalm 86:11-13

Love that Never Ceases

O Lord, give us,
we beseech Thee,
in the name of Jesus Christ,
that love which shall never cease,
that will kindle our lamps
but not extinguish them,
that they may enlighten others
and may always desire Thee.

∾ *St. Columba* ∾

Fulfill in Us Thy Purpose

O Lord Jesus Christ
our Maker and Redeemer,
Thy providence hast made us
what we are:
Thou hast a purpose for us;
Do Thou, O Lord, in Thy mercy,
fulfill in us Thy purpose.
Thou alone art wisdom;
Thou knowest what may benefit
sinners such as we are;
Do Thou, in Thy mercy,
direct our future according to Thy will,
as seemeth best in the eyes
of Thy Majesty, O Jesus Christ, our Lord.

⌁ Henry VI ⌁

Strength

Father, hear the prayer we offer:
Not for ease that prayer shall be,
but for strength that we may ever
Live our lives courageously.
Be our strength in hours of weakness,
In our wanderings be our guide;
Through endeavor, failure, danger,
Father, be Thou at our side.

Love Maria Willis

Teach Us, Lord

Guide us,
teach us,
and strengthen us,
O Lord, we beseech Thee,
until we become as Thou
would'st have us to be:
pure, gentle, truthful,
high-minded, courteous, generous,
able, dutiful, and useful;
for Thy honor and glory.

Charles Kingsley

Seeking the Lord

Jesus, the very thought of Thee
With sweetness fills my breast;
But sweeter far Thy face to see,
And in Thy presence rest.

∽ Bernard of Clairvaux ∽

My heart says of you, "Seek his face!"
Your face, LORD, I will seek.

∽ Psalm 27:8 ∽

Spiritual Growth

Lead us from death to life,
from falsehood to truth.
Lead us from despair to hope,
from fear to trust.
Lead us from hate to love,
from war to peace.
Let peace fill our heart,
our world, our universe.

Anglican Prayer

To Love Him
Above All Things

O God, who hast prepared
for them that love Thee
such good things
as pass man's understanding;
Pour into our hearts
such love toward Thee,
that we, loving Thee
above all things,
may obtain Thy promises,
which exceed all that we can desire;
through Jesus Christ our Lord.
Amen
⌒ The Book of Common Prayer ⌒

God's Love

Love divine, all loves excelling,
Joy of Heaven, to earth come down,
Fix in us Thy humble dwelling,
All Thy faithful mercies crown;
Jesu, Thou art all compassion,
Pure unbounded love Thou art;
Visit us with Thy salvation,
Enter every trembling heart.

Charles Wesley

Touched By the Lord

You called,
You cried,
You shattered my deafness.
You sparkled,
You blazed,
You drove away my blindness.
You shed Your fragrance,
and I drew in my breath,
and I pant for You.
I tasted and now
I hunger and thirst.
You touched me,
and now I burn
with longing for Your peace.

◾ *Augustine of Hippo* ◾

May **Love Abound**

I thank my God
every time I remember you.
In all my prayers for all of you,
I always pray with joy
because of your partnership in the gospel
from the first day until now,
being confident of this,
that he who began a good work in you
will carry it on to completion
until the day of Christ Jesus.
It is right for me to feel this way
about all of you,
since I have you in my heart;
for whether I am in chains
or defending and confirming the gospel,
all of you share in God's grace with me.

God can testify how I long for all of you
with the affection of Christ Jesus.
And this is my prayer:
that your love may abound
more and more in knowledge
and depth of insight,
so that you may be able to discern
what is best and may be pure
and blameless until the day of Christ,
filled with the fruit of righteousness
that comes through Jesus Christ –
to the glory and praise of God.

Philippians 1:3-11

The Depth of His Love

I pray that out of his glorious riches he may strengthen you with power through his Spirit in your inner being, so that Christ may dwell in your hearts through faith.

And I pray that you, being rooted and established in love, may have power, together with all the saints, to grasp how wide and long and high and deep is the love of Christ, and to know this love that surpasses knowledge – that you may be filled to the measure of all the fullness of God.

Now to him who is able to do immeasurably more than all we ask or imagine, according to his power that is at work within us, to him be glory in the church and in Christ Jesus throughout all generations, for ever and ever!

Amen

Ephesians 3:16-21

Spirit of Life and Love

Come! Spirit of Love!
Penetrate and transform us
by the action of Your purifying life.
May Your constant, brooding love
bring forth in us more love
and all the graces
and works of love.
Give us grace to remain
still under its action,
and may the humble stillness
be our prayer.
Amen

Evelyn Underhill

Love's Lesson

Savior, teach me, day by day,
Love's sweet lesson to obey;
Sweeter lesson cannot be,
Loving Him who first loved me.
With a childlike heart of love,
At Your bidding may I move;
Prompt to serve and follow Thee,
Loving Him who first loved me.
Teach me all Your steps to trace,
Strong to follow in Your grace,
Learning how to love from Thee,
Loving Him who first loved me.
Thus may I rejoice to show
That I feel the love I owe;
Singing, till Your face I see,
Of His love who first loved me.

⏤ Jane Leeson ⏤

Wisdom in Speech

O Jesus,
Son of God,
who was silent before Pilate,
do not let us wag our tongues
without thinking of what we are to say
and how to say it.

Irish Prayer

Service
and
Ministry

A Life to Proclaim Him

O gracious and holy Father,
give us wisdom to perceive Thee,
intelligence to understand Thee,
diligence to seek Thee,
patience to wait for Thee,
eyes to behold Thee,
a heart to meditate upon Thee,
and a life to proclaim Thee;
through the power of the Spirit
of Jesus Christ our Lord.

St. Benedict

Purity

Almighty God,
unto whom all hearts be open,
all desires known,
and from whom no secrets are hid;
cleanse the thoughts of our hearts
by the inspiration of Thy Holy Spirit,
that we may perfectly love Thee
and worthily magnify Thy holy name.
Through Christ our Lord.
Amen

The Book of Common Prayer

May **All** I Bring

My life I bring to Thee,
I would not be my own;
O Savior, let me be
Thine ever, Thine alone.
My heart, my life, my all I bring
To Thee, my Savior and my King.

Frances Havergal

Breathe on Me, Breath of God

Breathe on me, Breath of God;
Fill me with life anew,
That I may love what Thou dost love,
And do what Thou wouldst do.
Breathe on me, Breath of God,
Till I am wholly Thine,
Until this earthly part of me
Glows with Thy fire divine.

~ Edwin Hatch ~

An Un**divided** Heart

Teach me Your ways, O Lord my God,
And I will walk in Your truth;
Give me a totally undivided heart;
Cleanse me, Lord, I pray;
Remove from me all that is
standing in the way of Your love.

⤳ *Eugene Greco* ⤳

Doing Good

Dear Lord,
I shall pass through this world but once;
any good, therefore, that I can do
or any kindness that I can show to any
fellow creature
let me do it now;
let me not defer or neglect it,
for I shall not pass this way again.

Stephen Grellet

Stillness

We are so busy, Lord,
we do not listen.
The world is so noisy, Lord,
we do not hear.
We do not hear what Your Spirit
is saying to each one of us.
We have been afraid of silence.
Lord, teach us to use Your gift of silence.
Teach us, Lord.

Unknown

Moment by Moment

My life is an instant,
an hour which passes by;
My life is a moment
which I have no power to stay.
You know, O my God,
that to love You here on earth –
I have only today.

Thérèse of Lisieux

My Small Life

Lord!
Come in!
Enter my small life!
Lay Your sacred hands on all the common
things and small interests of that life and
bless and change them. Transfigure my
small resources, make them sacred. And
in them, give me Your very self.
Amen

∽ Evelyn Underhill ∽

I Desire to do Your Will

Lord,
You know what I desire,
but I desire it only
if it is Your will
that I should have it.
If it is not Your will,
good Lord,
do not be displeased,
for my will is to do Your will.

Julian of Norwich

A Humble Heart

Thy home is with the humble, Lord,
The simple are Thy rest;
Thy lodging is in childlike hearts;
Thou makest there Thy nest.

~ F. W. Faber ~

Reflect the Lord's Image

Lord, make my soul
to mirror Thee,
Thyself alone
to shine in me,
that men may see
Thy love, Thy grace,
nor note the glass
that shows Thy face.
— Blanche Kelly —

Lives Used by Thee

O Lord our God, we offer to Thee
our hearts and our minds,
our wills and our work.
Fill us with Thy Spirit that our lives may
be used by Thee.
Amen

⟡ Unknown ⟡

The Will of God

Blessed Master,
with my whole heart I thank You
for the wonderful lesson
that the path to a life of answers
to prayer is through the will of God.
Lord, teach me to know
this blessed will by living it,
loving it, and always doing it.
So shall I learn to offer prayers
according to that plan,
and to find in harmony
with Your blessed will
my boldness in prayer
and my confidence
in accepting the answer.

Andrew Murray

The Light of His Spirit

Open wide the windows of our spirits,
O Lord, and fill us full of light;
open wide the door of our hearts, that we
may receive and entertain Thee with all
our powers of adoration and love.

~ *Christina Rossetti* ~

Rejoice in Who I Am

I do not know when I have had
happier times in my soul,
than when I have been sitting at work,
with nothing before me
but a candle and a white cloth,
and hearing no sound
but my own breath,
with You in my soul
and heaven in my eye.
I rejoice in being exactly what I am –
a creature capable of loving You
and who, as long as I live, must be happy.
I get up and look for a while
out of the window
and gaze at the moon and stars,
the work of Your Almighty hand.
I think of the grandeur of the universe
and then sit down and think myself
one of the happiest beings in it.

Unknown (18th century)

Blessings of Delight

Let us bow our souls and say, "Behold the handmaid of the Lord!" Let us lift up our heart and ask, "Lord, what wouldst Thou have me to do?" Then the light from the opened heaven shall stream on our daily task, revealing the grains of gold, where yesterday all seemed dust. A hand shall sustain us and our daily burden, so that, smiling at yesterday's fears, we shall say, "This is easy, this is light"; every "lion in the way", as we come up to it, shall be seen chained, and leave open the gates of the Palace Beautiful; and to us, even to us, feeble and fluctuating as we are, ministries shall be assigned, and through our hands blessings shall be conveyed in which the spirits of just men made perfect might delight.

⊸ Elizabeth Charles ⊸

To Do All Things for God

Teach me, my God and king,
in all things Thee to see,
that what I do in anything
to do it as for Thee.

         ∽ *George Herbert* ∽

Joy in Giving

Make us ever eager, Lord,
to share the good things that we have.
Grant us such a measure
of Thy Spirit that we may find
more joy in giving than in getting.
Make us ready to give
cheerfully without grudging,
secretly without praise,
and in sincerity
without looking for gratitude,
for Jesus' Christ's sake.
Amen

∾ *John Hunter* ∾

To Share the Love of God

Oh teach me, Lord, that I may teach
the precious things Thou dost impart;
And wing my words, that they may reach
the hidden depths of many a heart.
Oh fill me with Thy fullness, Lord,
until my very heart o'erflow
in kindling thought and glowing word,
Thy love to tell, Thy praise to show.
Oh use me, Lord, use even me.
Just as Thou wilt, and when, and where,
until Thy blessed face I see,
Thy rest, Thy joy, Thy glory share.

— Frances Havergal —

Joy and Serenity

Grant us, O Lord,
the royalty of inward happiness
and the serenity that comes
from living close to Thee.
Daily renew in us the sense of joy,
and let Thy eternal Spirit dwell
in our souls and bodies,
filling every corner of our hearts
with light and gladness.
So that, bearing about with us
the infection of a good courage,
we may be diffusers of life,
and meet all that comes,
of good or ill, even death itself,
with gallant and high-hearted happiness;
giving Thee thanks always for all things.

— Robert Louis Stevenson —

Commitment to Service

Lord Jesus, take me this day and use me.
Take my lips and speak through them.
Take my mind and think through it.
Take my will and act through it,
and fill my heart with love for You.

⌒ Traditional ⌒

Let My Light Shine

Dear Jesus, help me to spread
Your fragrance everywhere I go.
Flood my soul with Your Spirit and life.
Penetrate and possess
my whole being so utterly,
that my life may only be
a radiance of Yours.
Shine through me, and be so in me,
that every soul I come in contact with
may feel Your presence in my soul.
Let them look up and see no longer me,
but only Jesus!
Stay with me, and then I shall begin to
shine as You shine;
so to shine as to be a light to others.

John Henry Newman

Use Your Gifts
for His Glory

O Lord our God,
give us by Your Holy Spirit
a willing heart and a ready hand
to use all Your gifts
to Your praise and glory;
through Jesus Christ our Lord.
Amen

⸺ Thomas Cranmer ⸺

The Needs of Others

O Lord,
Open my eyes that I may see
the needs of others;
open my ears
that I may hear their cries;
open my heart
so that they need not be without succor;
Let me not be afraid
to defend the weak
because of the anger of the strong,
nor afraid to defend
the poor because of the anger of the rich.
Show me where love
and hope and faith are needed,
and use me to bring them
to these places.
And so open my eyes
and my ears that I may
this coming day be able
to do some work of peace for Thee.

                    ∽ *Alan Paton* ∽

The Work of Today

O Living God!
Help us to appreciate
the present moment
and to search out its advantages
that we may be glad
for the todays of life,
leaving the tomorrows in Thy hand.
Steady us to do our full stint of work.
Help us to rise
each day with new sympathies,
new thoughts of unity and joy.

Helen Keller

Delightful Praise

Lord, with what courage and delight
I do each thing,
When Thy least breath sustains my wing;
I shine and move
Like those above,
And with much gladness
Quitting sadness,
Make me fair days of every night.

⌐ Henry Vaughan ⌐

Love for the People of the World

Tonight I ask You to help me to love.
Grant me, Lord,
to spread true love in the world.
Grant that by me and by Your children
it may penetrate a little into all circles,
all societies, all economic and political
systems, all laws, all contacts, all rulings;
Grant that it may penetrate
into offices, factories, apartment
buildings, cinemas, dance-halls;
Grant that it may penetrate the hearts of
men and that I may never forget that the
battle for a better world is a battle of love,
in the service of love.
Help me to love, Lord,
not to waste my powers of love,
to love myself less and less in order to
love others more and more.

⟍ Michel Quoist ⟍

Help for Daily Living

Dear God,
You constantly pour out Your blessings
on us: help us to be a blessing to others.
You gave us our hands: help us to use
them to work for You.
You gave us our feet: help us to use them
to walk in Your ways.
You gave us our voices: help us to use
them to speak gentleness and truth.
You gave us our minds: help us to think
only pleasant, kind thoughts.
You have made our lives pleasant every
day with love: help us to make others'
lives happier every day with our love.
Help us to please You, Lord. Help us to
learn; some little deed to thank You with,
instead of words; some little prayer to do
instead of say; some little thing to give
You because You never tire of giving us
so much.
Amen

Unknown

Daily Duty

Cheered by the presence of God, I will
do at each moment, without anxiety,
according to the strength which He shall
give me, the work that His providence
assigns me. I will leave the rest without
concern; it is not my affair. I ought to
consider the duty to which I am called
each day, as the work that God has
given me to do, and to apply myself to it
in a manner worthy of His glory, that
is to say with exactness and in peace.

⁓ François Fénelon ⁓

Petition
and
Supplication

The Gift of the New Day

We give Thee hearty thanks
for the rest of the past night,
and for the gift of a new day,
with its opportunities of pleasing Thee.
Grant that we may so pass
the hours in the perfect freedom
of Thy service,
that at eventide we may again
give thanks unto Thee;
through Jesus Christ our Lord.
Amen

Third Century Prayer

Abundant Mercy

Almighty and everlasting God,
who art always more ready
to hear than we to pray,
and art wont to give more
than either we desire or deserve:
Pour down upon us
the abundance of Thy mercy;
forgiving us those things
whereof our conscience is afraid,
and giving us those good things
which we are not worthy to ask,
but through the merits
and mediation of Jesus Christ,
Thy Son, our Lord.
Amen

The Book of Common Prayer

Each Day's Need

And may these words of mine,
which I have prayed before the LORD,
be near to the LORD our God
day and night,
that he may uphold the cause
of his servant according
to each day's need,
so that all the peoples of the earth
may know that the LORD is God
and that there is no other.

1 Kings 8:59-60

For Grace

O Lord our heavenly Father,
Almighty and everlasting God,
who hast safely brought us
to the beginning of this day:
Defend us in the same
with Thy mighty power;
and grant that this day we fall into no sin,
neither run into any kind of danger;
but that all our doings
may be ordered by Thy governance,
to do always what is righteous
in Thy sight;
through Jesus Christ our Lord.
Amen

⟿ The Book of Common Prayer ⟿

A Diligent Spirit

Into Thy hands, O Lord,
we commit ourselves this day.
Give to each one of us a watchful,
a humble, and a diligent spirit,
that we may seek in all things
to know Thy will,
and when we know it
may perform it perfectly and gladly,
to the honor and glory of Thy name,
through Jesus Christ our Lord.

⤍ Fifth Century Prayer ⤎

Protection from the Snares of the World

O Lord seek us, O Lord find us
in Thy patient care,
be Thy love before us, behind us,
round us everywhere.
Lest the god of this world blind us,
lest he bait a snare,
lest he forge a chain to bind us,
lest he speak us fair,
turn not from us, call to mind us,
find, embrace us, hear.
Be Thy love before us, behind us,
round us everywhere.
Christina Rossetti

Whitsunday

Come, Holy Spirit,
fill the hearts of Your faithful.
And kindle in them
the fire of Your love.
Send forth Your Spirit
and they shall be created
and You shall renew
the face of the earth.

∽ *Traditional Prayer on Whitsunday* ∽
(from Psalm 104:30)

Guidance

Show me your ways, O LORD,
teach me your paths;
guide me in your truth and teach me,
for you are God my Savior,
and my hope is in you all day long.
Remember, O LORD,
your great mercy and love,
for they are from of old.
Remember not the sins of my youth
and my rebellious ways;
according to your love remember me,
for you are good, O LORD.

Psalm 25:4-7

A Call for Mercy

Hear, O LORD, and answer me,
for I am poor and needy.
Guard my life,
for I am devoted to you.
You are my God;
save your servant who trusts in you.
Have mercy on me, O LORD,
for I call to you all day long.
Bring joy to your servant,
for to you, O LORD, I lift up my soul.
You are forgiving and good, O LORD,
abounding in love to all who call to you.
Hear my prayer, O LORD;
listen to my cry for mercy.
In the day of my trouble I will call to you,
for you will answer me.
Among the gods
there is none like you, O LORD;
no deeds can compare with yours.

All the nations you have made will come
and worship before you, O LORD;
they will bring glory to your name.
For you are great
and do marvelous deeds;
you alone are God.
Teach me your way, O LORD,
and I will walk in your truth;
give me an undivided heart,
that I may fear your name.
I will praise you, O LORD my God,
with all my heart;
I will glorify your name forever.
For great is your love toward me;
you have delivered me
from the depths of the grave.

Psalm 86:1-13

Daily Petition

O Giver of each perfect gift!
This day our daily bread supply;
While from the Spirit's tranquil depths
We drink unfailing draughts of joy.

Lyra Catholica

The Path of Life

Lord, lover of Life,
remember Your creation for good,
for we are Yours.
Christ died and came to life again
to establish His lordship
over dead and living:
Whether therefore we live or die
we belong to You.
Father, by the raising of Christ
from the dead,
set our feet on the path of new life,
show us where we have
followed the path of death,
and give us every good thing we need
to do Your will.
Have mercy on us, Lord.
Bless us and watch over us,
be gracious to us,
look kindly on us and give us peace.

Launcelot Andrewes

For My Friends

Almighty, everlasting God, have mercy on Thy servants our friends. Keep them continually under Thy protection, and direct them according to Thy gracious favor in the way of everlasting salvation; that they may desire such things as please Thee, and with all their strength perform the same. And forasmuch as they trust in Thy mercy, vouchsafe, O Lord, graciously to assist them with Thy heavenly help, that they may ever diligently serve Thee, and by no temptations be separated from Thee; through Jesus Christ our Lord.

⊸ Thomas à Kempis ⊸

God's **Will** Day by Day

Almighty God,
help us to do Thy will
in our homes day by day,
that love and peace,
with all other graces,
may live and grow among us;
through Jesus Christ our Lord.

To Thine eternal faithfulness and love,
O God our Father,
we commend ourselves
and all who are dear to us.
And unto Thee be all glory and praise
from the whole Church
of Jesus Christ, world without end.
Amen.

Unknown

At Day's End

O Lord my God, thank You
for bringing this day to a close;
Thank You for giving
me rest in body and soul.
Your hand has been over me
and has guarded and preserved me.
Forgive my lack of faith
and any wrong that I have done today,
and help me to forgive
all who have wronged me.
Let me sleep in peace
under Your protection,
and keep me
from the temptations of darkness.
Into Your hands
I commend my loved ones
and all who dwell in this house.
I commend to You my body and soul.
O God, Your holy name be praised.
Amen

Dietrich Bonhoeffer

For Peace

O God,
Who art Peace everlasting,
whose chosen reward is the gift of peace,
and who hast taught us
that the peacemakers are Thy children,
pour Thy sweet peace into our souls,
that everything discordant
may utterly vanish,
and all that makes for peace
be sweet to us forever.

Gelasian

Home
and
Family

For My Child

Defend, O Lord,
this Thy child
with Thy heavenly grace,
that he may continue Thine forever;
and daily increase
in Thy Holy Spirit,
more and more,
until he come
unto Thy everlasting Kingdom.
Amen

⟝ The Book of Common Prayer ⟞

God's Presence
in Daily Tasks

O God,
Thou art with me
and it is Thy will
that these outward tasks
are given me to do.
Therefore, I ask Thee,
assist me,
and through it all
let me continue in Thy presence.
Be with me in this my endeavor,
accept the labor of my hands,
fill my heart as always.

Brother Lawrence

A Prayer of
Blessing and Petition

Have mercy,
O most gracious God,
upon all men.
Bless especially my father and mother,
my brothers and sisters,
my relatives and friends
and all whom I love
or who are kind to me.
Bless also the clergy of this parish,
have pity upon the sick and suffering.
Give us food and clothing,
keep us in good health,
comfort us in all our troubles,
make us to please Thee in all we do
and bring us safe at last
to our home in heaven:
Through Jesus Christ our Lord.
Amen

Charles Boyd

Grace Before Meals

Be present at our table, Lord
be here and everywhere adored.
His mercies bless and grant that we
may strengthened for Thy service be.
Amen

Traditional grace

A Kitchen Prayer

Bless my kitchen, Lord,
I love its every nook
and bless me as I do my work
wash pots and pans and cook.
May the meals that I prepare
be seasoned from above
with Thy blessing and Thy grace
but most of all Thy love.
As we partake of earthly food,
the table Thou hast spread,
we'll not forget to thank Thee, Lord,
for all our daily bread.
So bless my kitchen, Lord,
and those who enter in.
May they find naught but joy and peace
and happiness therein.

Unknown

A Prayer for Absent Family

We thank Thee, O Lord,
that Thou art in every place,
that no space or distance
can ever separate us from Thee.
That those who are absent
from one another
are still present in Thee.
Have in Thy holy keeping
all those from whom we are separated
and grant that we,
by drawing closer to Thee,
may be drawn closer to each other.
Amen

Unknown

To Pray with Children as They Go to Bed

Jesus, tender Shepherd, hear me,
bless Thy little lamb tonight,
through the darkness be Thou near me,
keep me safe till morning light.
Through this day Thy hand has led me,
and I thank Thee for Thy care.
Thou hast clothed me,
warmed and fed me,
listen to my evening prayer.
Let my sins be all forgiven,
bless the friends I love so well;
take me, when I die, to heaven,
happy there with Thee to dwell.

Mary Duncan

For Those Who Tend Children

O God,
We pray for all those
who have the privilege
and responsibility of nurturing
the children of this world.
May they be conscious
of the task entrusted to them
to enable each child
to grow and develop in mind,
in body, and in spirit.
May they encourage
each young person
to find the gifts
You have given them
and work so that every home
is touched by Christ.

Christine Eames

A Blessed Family

Lord, behold our family here assembled;
we thank Thee
for this place in which we dwell,
for the love that unites us,
for the peace accorded us this day,
for the hope
with which we expect the morrow.
For the health, the work,
the food, and the bright skies
that make our lives delightful.
For our friends in all parts of the earth ...
Give us courage
and gaiety and the quiet mind.

Bless us, if it may be,
in all our innocent endeavors.
If it may not,
give us the strength to encounter
that which is to come,
that we may be brave in peril,
constant in tribulation,
temperate in wrath.
And in all changes of fortune
and down to the gate of death
loyal and loving to one another.
As the clay to the potter
as the windmill to the wind
as children of their sire –
we beseech of Thee this help and mercy
for Christ's sake.

Robert Louis Stevenson

Bless This Home

Visit, we beseech Thee, O Lord,
our homes and drive from them
the snares of the enemy:
let Thy holy angels dwell therein
to preserve us in peace:
and may Thy blessing
be upon us evermore;
through Jesus Christ our Lord.
Amen

The Book of Common Prayer

The Sanctity of the Home

O God of all the families of men,
we commend unto Thee
every home in this land.
Preserve to us
the sanctities of family life,
and unite parents and children
in true affection
to one another and to Thee.
Give wisdom to all
Christian parents and teachers,
that they may bring up their children
in true faith and obedience to Thy Word.
Take our children
into Thy loving care,
that they may be kept from evil
and grow daily in good;
through Jesus Christ our Lord.
Amen

Unknown

Raising Small Children

For all these smallnesses
I thank You, Lord:
small children
and small needs;
small meals to cook,
small talk to heed,
and a small book
from which to read
small stories;
small hurts to heal,
small disappointments, too,
as real
as ours;
small glories
to discover
in bugs, pebbles, flowers.
When day is through my mind is small,
my strength is gone;
and as I gather
each dear one
I pray, "Bless each

for Jesus' sake –
such angels sleeping,
imps awake!"
What wears me out
are little things:
angels minus
shining wings.
Forgive me, Lord,
if I have whined:
it takes so much
to keep them shined;
yet each small rub
has its reward,
for they have blessed me.
Thank You,
Lord.

Ruth Graham

For the Children

Father, hear us, we are praying,
hear the words our hearts are saying,
we are praying for our children.
Keep them from the powers of evil,
from the secret, hidden, peril,
from the whirlpool
that would suck them,
from the treacherous quicksand
pluck them.
From the worldlings' hollow gladness,
from the sting of faithless sadness,
Holy Father, save our children.
Through life's troubled waters steer them,
through life's bitter battle cheer them,
Father, Father, be Thou near them.
Read the language of our longing,
read the wordless pleadings thronging,
Holy Father, for our children.
And wherever they may bide,
lead them home at eventide.

Amy Carmichael

At Bedtime

Lord, through this night
may we be in Thy keeping,
send Thou Thy heavenly host
to guard us sleeping.
O Light of lights,
be Thou our Light divine
and in our darkest hour –
Lord keep us Thine.

The Royal Naval College Hymnbook

Facing
Difficulties

When Dark Clouds Gather

My God! in whom are all the springs
of boundless love and grace unknown,
hide me beneath Thy spreading wings,
till the dark cloud is o'erblown.

⌐Isaac Watts ⌐

Through the Storm

Take my hand,
precious Lord,
lead me on,
let me stand.
I am tired, I am weak, I am worn.
Through the storm,
through the night,
lead me on to the light.
Take my hand,
precious Lord,
lead me home.

~ Thomas Dorsey ~

Psalm 23

The LORD is my shepherd, I
    shall not be in want.
He makes me lie down in
    green pastures,
he leads me beside quiet
    waters,
    he restores my soul.
He guides me in paths of
    righteousness
    for his name's sake.
Even though I walk
    through the valley of the
    shadow of death,
I will fear no evil,
    for you are with me;
    your rod and your staff,
    they comfort me.

You prepare a table before me
   in the presence of my
      enemies.
You anoint my head with oil;
   my cup overflows.
Surely goodness and love will
      follow me
   all the days of my life,
and I will dwell in the house of
      the Lord forever.

Psalm 23

When You Don't Know What to Do

Being perplexed, I say,
>   Lord, make it right!
>   Night is as day to Thee,
>   darkness is as light.
I am afraid to touch things that involve so much –
>   My trembling hand may shake,
>   my skill-less hand may break:
>   Thine can make no mistake.

~ Anna Warner ~

More **Than** Conquerors

Who shall separate us from the love of Christ? Shall trouble or hardship or persecution or famine or nakedness or danger or sword? As it is written: "For your sake we face death all day long; we are considered as sheep to be slaughtered."

No, in all these things we are more than conquerors through him who loved us. For I am convinced that neither death nor life, neither angels nor demons, neither the present nor the future, nor any powers, neither height nor depth, nor anything else in all creation, will be able to separate us from the love of God that is in Christ Jesus our Lord.

Romans 8:35-39

Praise
and
Thanksgiving

The Gifts of God's Goodness

For this new morning and its light,
for rest and shelter of the night,
for health and food, for love and friends,
for every gift Your goodness sends,
we thank You, gracious Lord.

~ Unknown ~

God's Love and Joy

My God, I thank Thee, who has made
the earth so bright;
So full of splendor and of joy,
beauty and light;
So many glorious things are here,
noble and right.
I thank Thee too that Thou hast made
joy to abound;
So many gentle thoughts and deeds
circling us round,
that in the darkest spot on earth
some love is found.

Adelaide Procter

Pied Beauty

Glory be to God for dappled things –
For skies of couple-color
as a brinded cow;
For rose-moles
all in stipple upon trout that swim;
Fresh-firecoal chestnut-falls;
finches' wings;
Landscape plotted and pieced-fold,
fallow, and plough;
And, all trades, their gear and tackle trim.
All things counter,
original, spare, strange;
Whatever is fickle, freckled
 (who knows how?)
with swift, slow; sweet,
sour; adazzle, dim;
He fathers-forth whose beauty
is past change:
Praise Him.

Gerard Manley Hopkins

Thank You

Thank You, Lord, thank You.
Thank You for the tranquil night.
Thank You for the stars.
Thank You for the silence.
Thank You for the time
You have given me.
Thank You for life.
Thank You for grace.
Thank You for being there, Lord.
Thank You for listening to me, for taking
me seriously, for gathering my gifts in
Your hands to offer them to Your Father.
Thank You, Lord.
Thank You.
~ Michel Quoist ~

Hannah's Prayer

My heart rejoices in the LORD; in the LORD my horn is lifted high. My mouth boasts over my enemies, for I delight in your deliverance.

There is no one holy like the LORD; there is no one besides you; there is no Rock like our God.

Do not keep talking so proudly or let your mouth speak such arrogance, for the LORD is a God who knows, and by him deeds are weighed.

The bows of the warriors are broken, but those who stumbled are armed with strength. Those who were full hire themselves out for food, but those who were hungry hunger no more. She who was barren has borne seven children, but she who has had many sons pines away.

Praise and Thanksgiving

The LORD brings death and makes alive; he brings down to the grave and raises up. The LORD sends poverty and wealth; he humbles and he exalts. He raises the poor from the dust and lifts the needy from the ash heap; he seats them with princes and has them inherit a throne of honor.

For the foundations of the earth are the LORD's; upon them he has set the world. He will guard the feet of his saints, but the wicked will be silenced in darkness.

It is not by strength that one prevails; thoe who oppose the LORD will be shattered. He will thunder against them from heaven; the LORD will judge the ends of the earth.

He will give strength to his king and exalt the horn of his anointed.

1 Samuel 2:1-10

Mary's Song of Praise

My soul glorifies the Lord and my spirit rejoices in God my Savior, for he has been mindful of the humble state of his servant. From now on all generations will call me blessed, for the Mighty One has done great things for me– holy is his name. His mercy extends to those who fear him, from generation to generation.

He has performed mighty deeds with his arm; he has scattered those who are proud in their inmost thoughts. He has brought down rulers from their thrones but has lifted up the humble. He has filled the hungry with good things but has sent the rich away empty. He has helped his servant Israel, remembering to be merciful to Abraham and his descendants forever, even as he said to our fathers.

Luke 1:46-55

Praise the Lord

You are the great God –
He who is in heaven.
You are the Creator of life,
You make the regions above.
You are the hunter
who hunts for souls.
You are the leader who goes before us.
You are He
whose hands are with wounds.
You are He whose feet are with wounds.
You are He whose blood
is a trickling stream.
You are He whose blood
was spilled for us.

Unknown

Cup of Happiness

Lord God how full our cup of happiness!
We drink and drink –
and yet it grows not less;
but every morn the newly risen sun
finds it replenished, sparkling, overrun.
Hast Thou not given us raiment,
warmth, and meat,
and in due season all earth's fruit to eat?
Work for our hands
and rainbows for our eyes,
and for our souls,
the wings of butterflies?
A father's smile,
a mother's fond embrace,

the tender light upon a lover's face?
The talk of friends,
the twinkling eye of mirth,
the whispering silence
of the good green earth?
Hope for our youth
and memories for age,
and psalms
upon the heaven's moving page?
And dost Thou not of pain
a mingling pour,
to make the cup but overflow the more?

                                  ⮞ Gilbert Thomas ⮜

Ordinary Things

I bless Thee, O Father, for all the
seemingly ordinary things –
> a cup of tea at rising;
> a letter through the post;
> a bunch of flowers for my vase.

I would not take for granted any gift
which brings me joy –
> health and strength and good food;
> a walk with another in the
> sunshine;
> a favorite book passed on by a
> friend.

With Paul and people of every
generation, I join in saying that there is
nothing that can separate us –
neither height nor depth;
neither life nor death.
Thou art worthy of more love than I can
bring – accept what I do bring.

⟶ Rita Snowden ⟶

Praise His Holy Name

Praise the LORD, O my soul;
and my inmost being,
praise his holy name.
Praise the LORD, O my soul,
and forget not all his benefits –
who forgives all your sins
and heals all your diseases,
who redeems your life
from the pit and crowns you
with love and compassion,
who satisfies your desires
with good things
so that your youth
is renewed like the eagle's.

Psalm 103:1-5